CONTENTS

The Snow Maze
by Jan Mark,
illustrated by Jan Ormerod

CREDITS

Published by Scholastic Ltd,
Villiers House,
Clarendon Avenue,
Leamington Spa,
Warwickshire CV32 5PR
Text © Guy Merchant
© 1999 Scholastic Ltd
1 2 3 4 5 6 7 8 9 0   9 0 1 2 3 4 5 6 7 8

Author Guy Merchant
Editor Kate Pearce
Series designer Lynne Joesbury
Designer Clare Brewer
Illustrations Jan Ormerod
Cover illustration Jan Ormerod

Designed using Adobe Pagemaker

British Library Cataloguing-in-Publication Data
A catalogue record for this book is available
from the British Library.

ISBN 0-439-01688-6

ACKNOWLEDGEMENTS

A & C Black (Publishers) Ltd for the use of an
extract from *The Blob* by Tessa Potter © 1994, Tessa
Potter (1994 Chiller Series, A & C Black).
Laura Cecil Literary Agency for the use of
redrawn illustrations, previously unpublished, by
Jan Ormerod © 1999 Jan Ormerod.
Random House UK Ltd for the use of an extract
from *The Fantastic Maze Book* by Juliet and
Charles Snape © 1994 Juliet and Charles Snape
(1994, Julia MacRae Books).
Walker Books Ltd for the use of photographs,
text, covers and illustrations from *The Snow Maze*
by Jan Mark Text © 1992 Jan Mark. Illustrations ©
1992 Jan Ormerod (1992, Walker Books).

The author would like to thank:
Jan Mark for her comments on the writing of
The Snow Maze featured in Author's Views.
Jan Ormerod for her comments on the
illustrations for *The Snow Maze* featured in
Illustrator's Views.
Joe Atkinson and **Hannah** for their comments
on the activities.

I think and think on things impossible
Yet love to wander in that golden maze
Dryden

INTRODUCTION

The Snow Maze
by Jan Mark, illustrated by Jan Ormerod

JAN MARK

Jan Mark grew up in Kent. She began writing in 1973 and has written a large number of very successful books for children. She now lives in Oxford. This is what she says about *The Snow Maze*.

I was very interested in mazes when I wrote the book. Some mazes are very old indeed.

It's about following your own path – standing up to pressure – being an individual.

Making the sand maze is a bit of lateral thinking.

It's about trusting people. Joe will only trust Irrum if she can see the maze.

JAN ORMEROD

Jan Ormerod lives in Cambridge and has worked as an illustrator for a number of years. She has created many picture books including *101 Things to do with Baby* and *The True Story of Chicken Licken*. She also illustrates books for older readers. This is what she says about *The Snow Maze*.

I loved the idea and it was a visual gift so I agreed to illustrate it.

It's an older girl digging the maze, you see the maze has become public at this stage.

I'm intrigued by mazes – running a maze is a kind of special ritual.

What's it all about?

● Look at the front and back cover of *The Snow Maze*.

blurb   author   illustrator   title

review   spine   illustration

● Write down what you have found out about:

the cover picture _____

the author _____

the title of the book _____

the illustrator _____

the blurb _____

the review _____

the spine of the book _____

What's it all about (cont.)

● Now read the contents page and then flick through the whole book.

● What do you think the story is going to be about? Record your ideas in the table below. Use the sources column to say what gave you that idea. (Remember the work you did on the front and back cover.)

Ideas	Sources

Finding the key

● Read the first two pages of the story. Joe is the main character and he finds a special key. What might it open?

● Write your ideas in the boxes.

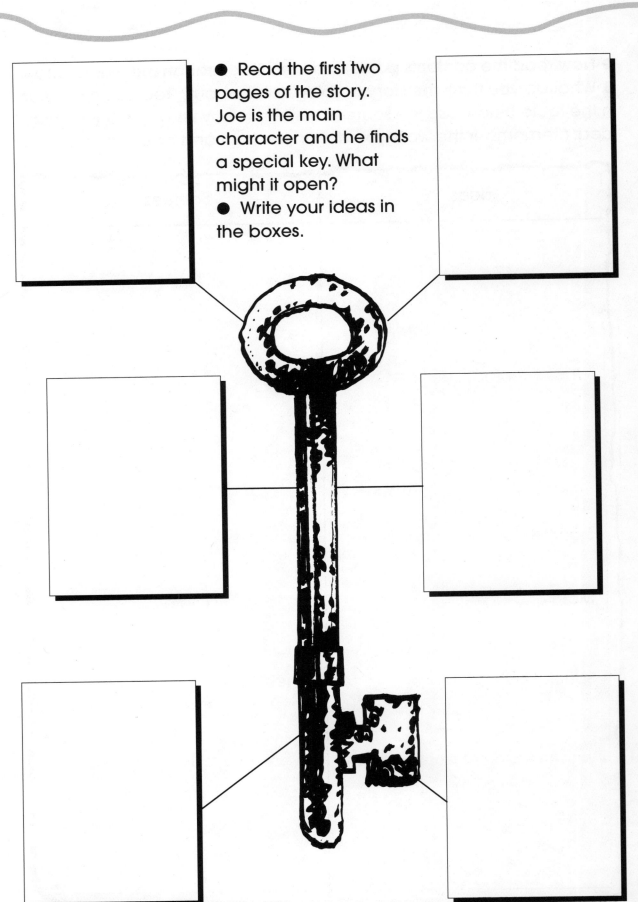

Special objects as story-starters

● Think of some stories you know in which the main character finds a special object. Write about them in the table below.

Story title: Main character: Special object: What the object does:	Story title: Main character: Special object: What the object does:
Story title: Main character: Special object: What the object does:	Story title: Main character: Special object: What the object does:

The key

● Read to the end of 'The Key' (Chapter 1). Think about what you know about Joe's key.

● Answer these questions (you can use phrases from the text and look at the illustrations to help you).

> **What does the key look and feel like?**

> **What do the children say about the key?**

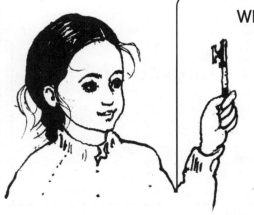

> **Why do you think Irrum says that the key might be magic?**

The lonely gate

● Read to the end of 'The Lonely Gate' (Chapter 2).
The adjective 'lonely' is normally used to describe people.
Write down some of the ways in which the gate
could be 'lonely'.

The gate could be lonely because

The gate could be lonely because

The gate could be lonely because

Perhaps Joe feels lonely too. Can you think why
Joe might be lonely?

Joe might be lonely because

Building tension

Read the following extract from 'The Lonely Gate'.

The gate was made of wood. Ivy climbed up it.
Joe moved the ivy leaves and underneath there was a keyhole. He put his key in the lock and turned it. The key clicked. The lock squeaked. Joe pushed. The ivy tried to hold shut the gate, but Joe pushed harder. The ivy let go. The hinges screeched. The gate opened.

What do you notice about the sentences that Jan Mark has used?
● Underline the sentences with three words in them.
● Underline the sentences with four words in them.

Short sentences can help to create tension and excitement in a story. Read the following extract from *The Blob* by Tessa Potter. Two children in this story are watching something strange going on.

Graham went first. I followed. I was sure I would be seen.
I ran as fast as I could. I just made it, but my heart was beating.
Then the main door opened slowly. It was Mr. Brown.

Notice how this author uses short sentences to create excitement.
● Underline two of the shortest sentences.
● Try this out for yourself. Write a few lines of your own about Joe finding the key. Use short sentences.

Maze talk

● Read to the end of 'The Lost Maze' (Chapter 3).
● In the classroom, people talk about mazes. Use the speech bubbles to show who says what about mazes.

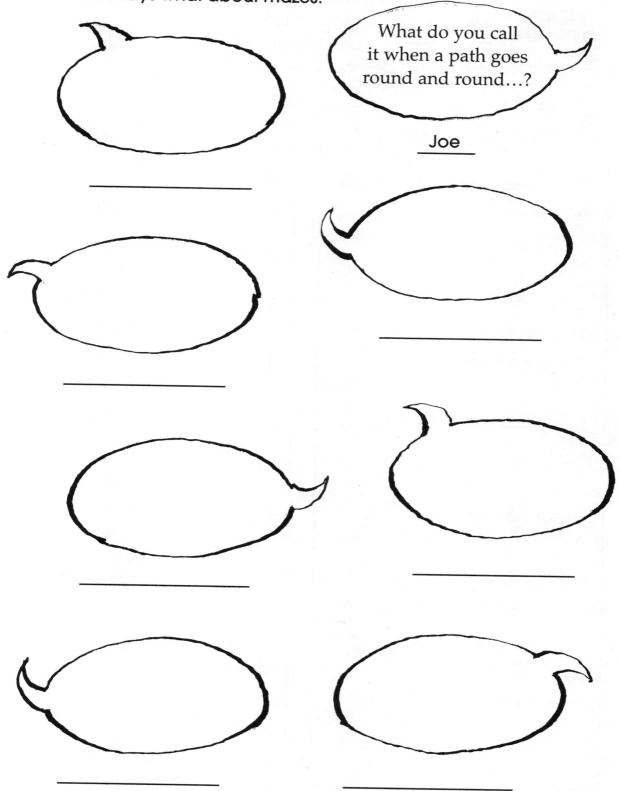

What do you call it when a path goes round and round…?

Joe

The characters

● Read 'The Secret Maze' (Chapter 4). This gives us more information about the children in the story and what they think about each other.

● Use the book to help you write some brief notes about Joe, Akash, Tim and Irrum. At the bottom of each box write up your notes into a brief description of each character.

Akash	Joe
Things it says about him in the book:	Things it says about him in the book:
Things he does:	Things he does:
Things he says:	Things he says:
He is	He is

The characters (cont.)

Tim	Irrum
Things it says about him in the book: Things he does: Things he says: He is	Things it says about her in the book: Things she does: Things she says: She is

Running rings round Joe

● Read 'The Invisible Maze' (Chapter 5).
Joe is being picked on because of the maze.
Other people make fun of him and this
makes Joe unhappy.

● How do the illustrations show that Joe is
being picked on? Make some notes.

When Joe is picked on at school he hides under the table and holds
his key. Imagine that his teacher sees him and tries to sort things out.
● Write a short playscript of a discussion between Joe and Miss.
You can continue on the back of this sheet.

MISS: Joe! Why are you hiding under the table?

JOE:

MISS:

JOE:

MISS:

JOE:

MISS:

How it all ends

● Read to the end of the book.
● The events below are jumbled up. Cut out the boxes and put them in the right order.

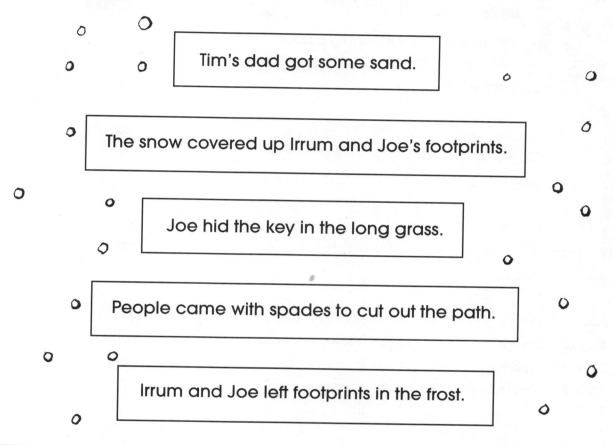

Tim's dad got some sand.

The snow covered up Irrum and Joe's footprints.

Joe hid the key in the long grass.

People came with spades to cut out the path.

Irrum and Joe left footprints in the frost.

Everyone was pleased that the children had found the lost maze.

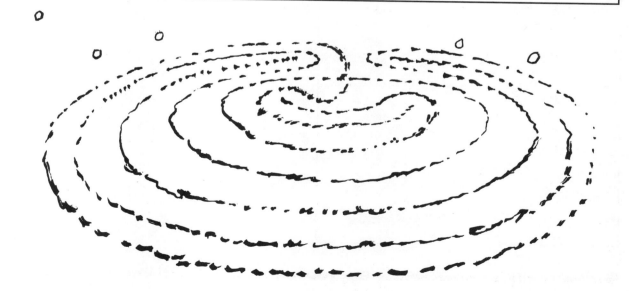

A-maze-ing

● Read the following paragraph from *The Fantastic Maze Book* by Juliet and Charles Snape.

A maze is a deliberately confusing series of paths or passages leading to a specific point, and designed to make life difficult, with lots of false turnings, dead ends and traps. Mazes are very ancient – in Greek mythology the Minotaur was imprisoned in a maze – and they can still sometimes be found in the gardens of great houses, like the famous maze at Hampton Court Palace.

● Make a list of the chapter titles from *The Snow Maze* on the chart below. Next to each one, note down the illustration or symbol that goes with it. One has been done for you.

Chapter title	Illustration
The Key	Joe kicking the key

● How do these illustrations help you to make sense of the story of *The Snow Maze.*

Joe's feelings

● Think about how Joe's feelings change at different points in the story. When do you think he is excited and happy? When does he feel sad and lonely?

● Write down how you imagine he thinks and feels at these different points in the story. Use the word bank at the bottom of the page to help you.

Joe finds the key. _____

Akash says "That key is no good." _____

Joe opens the gate. _____

Miss explains about the lost maze. _____

The children call him "Mazy, crazy, lazy Joe." _____

_____

Irrum sees the maze. _____

Everyone sees the maze. _____

Akash is pleased about the maze. _____

Joe hides the key. _____

excited	pleased	thoughtful	lonely
worried	anxious	disappointed	happy
scared	frightened	intrigued	afraid
fed up	glad	inspired	uncertain

Changing relationships

● Consider what Joe, Irrum and Akash thought about each other at the beginning of the book. (Look back at Chapter 1, 'The Key'.)

● Imagine what they thought about each other before this story starts. Did they know each other? Were they friends? How do their thoughts about each other change during the story?

● Write some notes about each character's thoughts in the chart below and on the next page.

Joe thinks	Irrum is	Akash is
Before the story		
After the first chapter		
After 'The Invisible Maze'		
At the end of the story		

Changing relationships (cont.)

Irrum thinks	Joe is	Akash is
Before the story		
After the first chapter		
After 'The Invisible Maze'		
At the end of the story		

Akash thinks	Irrum is	Joe is
Before the story		
After the first chapter		
After 'The Invisible Maze'		
At the end of the story		

It couldn't happen here

The Snow Maze is a magical fantasy. Many of the things in the story are familiar. Other things are unlikely to happen in reality.

● Look back through the story for familiar characters, places, objects and events. Make lists of these.

Characters
Irrum reminds me of

Places
Places in the book
remind me of

Objects
Some familiar objects
in the book are

Events
Some familiar events
in the story are

● Fantasy is about what is not likely to happen. Why do you think this story is called a magical fantasy? Write on the back of this sheet.

Sharing the maze

At the end of Chapter 4 the maze was Joe's 'secret'.
When Irrum wants to see the maze Joe says 'No' at first.

Why do you think Joe wants to keep his maze secret from Irrum?

What makes Joe change his mind?

How does Irrum persuade Joe to show the maze to the others?

Joe's secret diary

● Think about the events that take place from Chapter 5, 'The Invisible Maze', to the end of the story. Write down these events from Joe's point of view as diary entries.

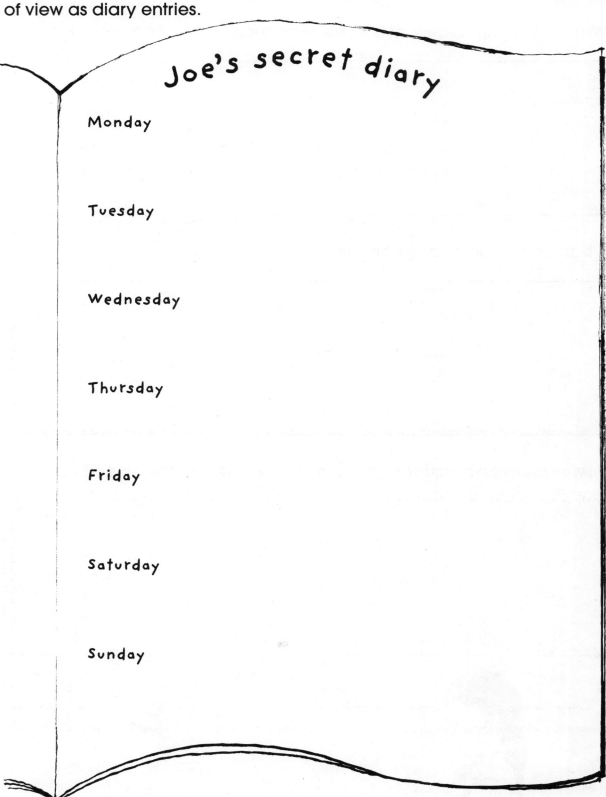

Joe's secret diary

Monday

Tuesday

Wednesday

Thursday

Friday

Saturday

Sunday

Maze time

Joe's teacher says to him:

> Once there was a turf maze near this school. But it was lost, long ago.

We know that the maze was there before Joe found it.

● Think of other things that might have happened before the story began. Make a list. For example: Who lost the key? What happened to make the wall fall down, leaving the lonely gate?

● Think of some things that might happen after the story ends. For example: Do Irrum and Joe continue to be friends? Make a list.

● Make a timeline showing the main events that happened before, during and after the story. You can use the back of this sheet.

Plotting events

The sentences in the boxes describe important events in the story.
● Cut them out and arrange them in the order in which they
happened. Glue the boxes onto the spiral in order. Stick the first event
on the outside and work your way to the centre.

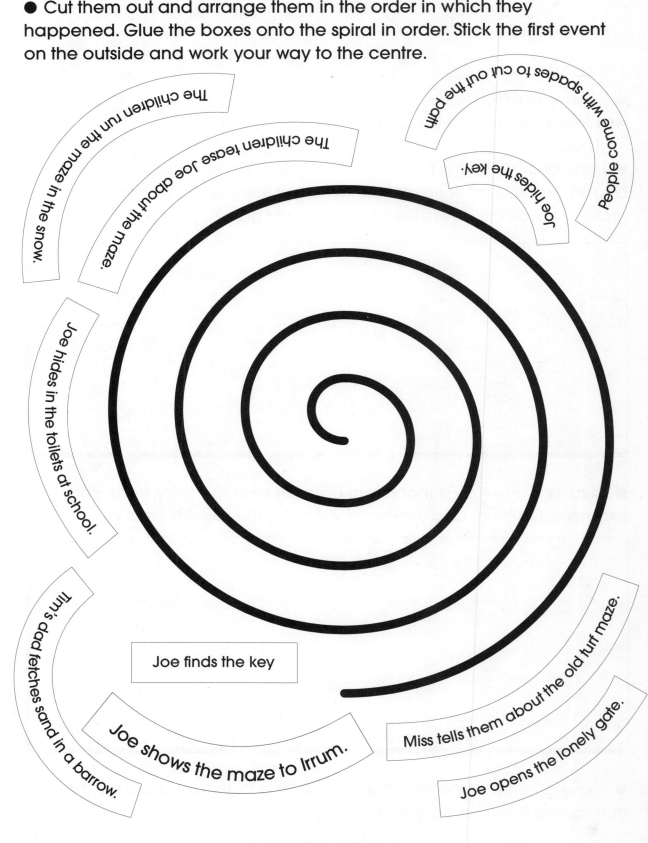

The children run the maze in the snow.

The children tease Joe about the maze.

People come with spades to cut out the path

Joe hides the key.

Joe hides in the toilets at school.

Tim's dad fetches sand in a barrow.

Joe finds the key

Joe shows the maze to Irrum.

Miss tells them about the old turf maze.

Joe opens the lonely gate.

Every picture tells a story

● Look closely at the picture of the children running round Joe.

Write a caption for this picture.

_____

● Look closely at the picture of the children running in the maze.

Write a caption for this picture.

_____

● Compare the two pictures. Both use silhouettes of the children. What are the differences?

● Choose another illustration from the book that you like and write a caption for it on the back of this sheet.

Thinking about the maze

- Look at what the author and illustrator say about *The Snow Maze*.
- What do they mean? Read each quote and write your ideas beside it.

Jan Mark says...	I think she means...
I was very interested in mazes when I wrote the book. Some mazes are very old indeed.	
It's about trusting people. Joe will only trust Irrum if she can see the maze.	
Making the sand maze is a bit of lateral thinking.	
It's about following your own path – standing up to pressure – being an individual.	
Jan Ormerod says...	**I think she means...**
I loved the idea and it was a visual gift so I agreed to illustrate it.	
I'm intrigued by mazes – running a maze is a kind of special ritual.	
It's an older girl digging the maze, you see the maze has become public at this stage.	

- What questions would you like to ask the author and illustrator? Write some questions on the back of this sheet.

The Snow Maze is a modern fantasy that explores the themes of loneliness and friendship. The story is based in a rural setting, and most of the main events take place on the children's journeys between home and school. The central character, Joe, finds a key which opens an old gate leading him to a magical maze. Both the key and the maze have a symbolic quality. At first no one else can see the maze, but later Irrum, who becomes Joe's confidante, shares the secret. As the story unfolds, Joe begins to trust and respect Irrum. Akash is a confident and popular boy who teases Joe about his 'invisible' maze. In the end footprints in the frost reveal the maze to everybody. Children run the maze in a snowfall, sand is poured onto their footprints and people come to cut out the turf maze for all to see. The story is short, simple in structure and uses everyday language. Jan Mark carefully encourages a reading that goes beyond the literal – one in which the maze, as an archetypal symbol, is seen as a metaphor for personal discovery and change.

MANAGING THE READING OF *THE SNOW MAZE*

The story is fairly short and so it is quite realistic to plan to re-read this book as a class novel or in individual reading time. This should be encouraged as it will help children to make sense of some of the deeper meanings of *The Snow Maze*. However, the activities in this book should be used to guide an initial reading of Jan Mark's book.

The author and illustrator are introduced on the first page and children should look at this before reading the book. The first two 'Ways in' activities (pages 4 and 5) encourage children to make predictions from the cover, illustration, blurb and contents page. The children read the first two pages and then complete the third activity about finding a key before reading on.

The activities in the 'Making sense' section are completed at various points during reading. Each activity relates to a particular chapter or group of chapters, as follows: 'The Key' – page 8; 'The Lonely Gate' – pages 9–10; 'The Lost Maze' – page 11; 'The Secret Maze' – pages 12–13; 'The Invisible Maze' – page 14; 'The Frost Maze' and 'The Sand Maze' – page 15.

The 'Developing ideas' activities encourage children to look at the story as a whole. This is where the distinctive features of the story are considered and where the story's themes are explored. Here, closer reading of written and visual elements of the book is important.

CLASSROOM MANAGEMENT AND SUPPORT

The Snow Maze is a short story that is quite simple to read. It lends itself well to group or individual reading, although it can, of course, be used with the whole class. If children have a tendency to race through their reading or to dismiss shorter stories as being 'babyish', this is a good choice. There is plenty of depth when we start thinking about Jan Mark's book. Try to ensure that the story is broken up with plenty of discussion about what has been read.

Children can work in pairs to complete the following activities: 'Special objects as story-starters' (page 7); 'Running rings round Joe' (page 14); 'Joe's feelings' (page 17) and 'Plotting events' (page 24). The following activities work well in a small group: 'The characters' (page 12–13) and 'Maze time' (page 23). Some of the activities ask children to re-read a particular part of the book. These are marked with the icon 📖. It is advisable to invest in at least six copies of *The Snow Maze* so that children can work independently or in groups. If the whole class is reading the book, plan so that some children are working from the text while others are doing activities that do not require direct access to a copy. Make sure that there is plenty of opportunity for children to give feed back and discuss the activities they have completed – either in groups or with the whole class.

TIME-SCALE

The story can easily be read aloud from cover to cover in about 15 minutes. This is one way of introducing the story after children have completed the 'Ways in' activities. Other activities will then encourage a closer reading. Alternatively you may choose to use a group reading approach, perhaps concluding with a whole-class read.

DIFFERENTIATION

All the activities in this book are designed so that they are accessible to Years 3 and 4 (P4 and 5) of primary school but could also be used in Year 5 and 6 (P6 and 7) classrooms. Be selective about the activities you use and when you use them. You may wish to use some of the 'Making sense' activities after the book has been read. Most of the activities will be differentiated by pupil response. Extension activities in the 'Teachers' notes' give ideas for extending the work further. Consideration should be given to children who may struggle with some of the material. Careful use of paired and group work can be useful, particularly in cases where children lack the confidence or motivation to record their thoughts. The core aims of each activity are provided in the 'Teachers' notes' section. The more challenging activities are: 'Special objects as story-starters', page 7; 'The characters', pages 12–13; 'Sharing the maze', page 21 and 'Maze time', page 23.

MATCHING THE BOOK TO YOUR CLASS

Although *The Snow Maze* is a short story, written in simple language, it introduces some mature themes about individuality and peer group pressure. This always provokes plenty of discussion and children can easily identify with the social issues that the book raises. Mazes themselves are fascinating, and they are a particularly rich area to research. They have historical as well as magical, religious and psychological significance.

TEACHING POTENTIAL OF *THE SNOW MAZE*

Extension activities are listed in the 'Teachers' notes', indicating further English activities as well as cross-curricular links.

Jan Mark is keen that children should draw or build a maze for themselves. This can be done as a model or full-scale (as suggested in the teachers' notes to 'Maze talk', see page 30). Children can do plenty of research into mazes using books and ICT material. There is a strong element of history here, as well as important geography work. The Mazemaker Internet site (http:// www.mazemaker.com) provides a database of mazes which you can use in map work. Other sites, as well as the more traditional adventure games, are based on puzzle mazes.

Links can also be made to PHSE through the exploration of bullying and teasing. Also, Jan Mark's idea of 'finding your own path' can be explored, particularly if the book is used in conjunction with *Taking the Cat's Way Home* (see 'Resources' below).

GLOSSARY

During the activities children will encounter some terminology which may be new to them. In talking about *The Snow Maze* you will need to check that they understand what is meant by 'author', 'illustrator', 'blurb' and the 'spine' of the book. When looking at the story, children will need an understanding of what we mean by 'fantasy', 'character', 'story-starter' and 'extract'. When talking about the language of the book, children will need to be clear about the terms 'sentence' and 'adjective'.

RESOURCES

The following books will support work with this text.

Some other books by Jan Mark
The Dead Letter Box (Penguin)
Dream House (Penguin)
Nothing to be Afraid Of (Penguin)
Trouble Half-way (Penguin)
Under the Autumn Garden (Penguin)
The Twig Thing (Penguin)
Taking the Cat's Way Home (Walker)

Some other books with illustrations by Jan Ormerod
101 Things to do with Baby (Penguin)
Sunshine (Viking)
The Story of Chicken Licken (Walker)

Other books for children
Willy the Wimp Anthony Browne (Walker Books)
Willy and Hugh Anthony Browne (Red Fox)
A Sudden Glow of Gold Anne Fine (Mammoth)
The Angel of Nitshill Road Anne Fine (Mammoth)
Boo! Colin McNaughton (Collins)
Captain Abdul's Pirate School Colin McNaughton (Walker)
The Wreck of the Zanzibar Michael Morpurgo (Mammoth)
The Blob Tessa Potter (Penguin)
The Fantastic Maze Book Juliet and Charles Snape (Random House)
Tigerella Kit Wright (Scholastic)

Sources for teachers
On mazes:
Secrets of the Maze: An Interactive Guide to the World's Most Amazing Mazes Adrian Fisher (Thames and Hudson)
Maze Patterns Aidan Meehan (Thames and Hudson)
Website: http//www.maze.maker.com
Larry's Party Carol Shields (Fourth Estate) – a novel with a strong maze theme and some good line drawings of mazes.
On bullying:
Bullying – Sorted! Zoe Crutchley and Veronica Parnell (Scripture Union)
How to Stop Bullying: A Kidscape Training Guide Michele Elliott and J Kirkpatrick (Kidscape)
On using drama:
Drama in Primary English Teaching Suzie Clipson-Boyles (David Fulton)
Drama – A Handbook for Primary Teachers Geof Readman and G. Lamont (BBC)
On using visual images and picture books:
Picture Books for the Literacy Hour Guy Merchant and Huw Thomas (David Fulton)
On terminology:
Reading and Responding to Fiction Huw Thomas (Scholastic)

WAYS IN
THE SNOW MAZE (PAGE 3)
Aim: to relate comments from the author and illustrator to the main themes and content of the book.

Teaching points: Jan Mark and Jan Ormerod's comments about *The Snow Maze* provide us with background information to the book. This information can be used at various stages in the reading. Jan Mark's comments on mazes will be useful during the reading of Chapter 3 ('The Lost Maze'). When looking at the illustrations in the activities 'A-maze-ing' page 16 and 'Every picture tells a story' page 25, you may want children to refer to page 3. Make a poster by enlarging the sheet to A3. Cut out the quotes and stick them to a poster-sized sheet of paper. The children can then illustrate it, and add comments and questions to it as they work their way through the book.

Extension: children can find out more about the author and illustrator. Use your local library service to build up a collection of works by Jan Mark. Use the quotes to try to work out the questions she was asked. This could lead to a role-play activity in which one child takes on the role of the author and another child that of an interviewer.

WHAT'S IT ALL ABOUT? (PAGE 4)
Aim: to make predictions about the story by studying the front and back cover.

Teaching points: if children are not already familiar with the terms used on the photocopiable sheet, introduce them during a class activity such as shared reading. Use another title by Jan Mark, such as *Taking the Cat's Way Home* or *The Twig Thing,* to model the activity.

Extension: children can review a variety of books and compare the type of information provided on the front and back covers and their responses to this. Discuss with the children how this influences their choice of book.

WHAT'S IT ALL ABOUT (CONT.) (PAGE 5)
Aim: to build on text predictions about the story by reading the contents page and skimming through the book.

Teaching points: check that children know how to find the contents page and what we mean by skimming through the book. A good way of introducing this is to demonstrate how you choose a book, thinking aloud as you do so. Bring in several books that you might read in order to illustrate this.

Extension: children can design posters for the book corner or the library on 'How to choose a book to read'. Encourage them to talk about visual features as well as content, choosing books on a theme, or books by authors and illustrators whose work they have enjoyed.

FINDING THE KEY (PAGE 6)
Aim: to identify the main character and the **inciting** moment (the discovery of the key), and to make predictions.

Teaching points: encourage children to go beyond single word answers. If the key opens a door, then what lies behind the door? If it's a cupboard, what's in the cupboard? and so on. If the children have read Oxford Reading Tree books, they will already be familiar with the idea of a magic key and how this unlocks further adventures, but remember at this stage there is no evidence to suggest that the key Joe finds is magic. The ideas could be explored as shared writing on story openings. This will also help as preparation for the following activity.

Extension: bringing in a collection of keys is a good way to get some storywriting going. Invite the caretaker in to show and talk about the school keys. Is there a key that doesn't seem to open anything?

SPECIAL OBJECTS AS STORY-STARTERS (PAGE 7)
Aim: to look at how some stories involve the discovery of a 'special' object (in this case a key) to develop the plot.

Teaching points: this activity may need a little discussion first. Talk about different objects such as a stone, a ring, a lantern or a magic carpet, which often have special powers in stories. Other stories which include examples of magical objects include *Aladdin, Jack and the Beanstalk, A Sudden Glow of Gold* (Anne Fine) or even *The Lord of the Rings.*

Extension: children could think of the role of special objects in television programmes, such as the Tardis in Dr Who, films and comics. They could also plan their own stories that feature the chance discovery of such an object. Ask them to think about *who* is in their story, *where* it takes place, *what* is the special object, and what *happens.*

MAKING SENSE
THE KEY (PAGE 8)
Aim: to look at the characteristics of an object in the story and the language that is used to describe it.

Teaching points: this activity follows on from the previous two activities, but by now the reader knows a bit more about the key. Encourage the children to refer to the illustrations as well as the text when doing this activity. Prompt the children to think about the way Joe counts five seconds: *"One-elephant, two elephant, three-elephant, four-elephant, five-elephant."* Is this just a good way of counting seconds or is it like a magic spell?

Extension: use a collection of keys as a stimulus for short pieces of descriptive writing. This can feed into a whole-class activity in which one child reads out a description of a particular key while the others have to work out which one is being described.

THE LONELY GATE (PAGE 9)

Aim: to look at the effect of using figurative language.

Teaching points: make sure the children are clear about the term 'adjective', since this is used on the photocopiable sheet. Discuss the difference between using literal and figurative descriptions. Read and discuss other stories, extracts or poems that use language in this way. Kit Wright's picture book *Tigerella* is an excellent introduction to this and is short enough to read in its entirety.

Extension: children can experiment with figurative language, using different adjectives to describe familiar places and objects. How is 'the angry playground' different from 'the cold playground' and so on.

BUILDING TENSION (PAGE 10)

Aim: to investigate the ways in which an author builds tension and excitement.

Teaching points: using short sentences is just one way of building up tension, but it is effective and Jan Mark uses the technique well. You could introduce this activity through a shared writing activity using short sentences to create excitement, or through the use of an extract like the one on the photocopiable sheet.

Extension: children could do a writing exercise to investigate the effect of sentence length, either redrafting some of their own writing or by working on an extract. You may like to use Colin McNaughton's *Boo!* to show how someone writing for a younger audience uses text layout and page breaks, as well as illustration and typeface, to create excitement.

MAZE TALK (PAGE 11)

Aim: to look at how information on a topic can be conveyed through dialogue.

Teaching points: we learn quite a lot about different kinds of mazes in this classroom discussion. Encourage the children to refer back to Jan Mark's own interest in mazes (see the author comments on page 3). Ask the children why they think Jan Mark is so interested in mazes – why should she want them to go and make their own maze after reading the story? The classroom discussion also tells us more about the characters: Miss is interested and knowledgeable; Tim draws on his own experience; Akash is dismissive, and

so on.

Extension: this is an ideal stepping-off point for background work and research on mazes and labyrinths. You can use fiction (the story of 'Theseus and the Minotaur' for example) as well as non-fiction sources. Let the children search for mazes on the Internet and using a computer-based encyclopaedia. If you cannot visit a maze, encourage children to investigate them as they occur in computer games and puzzles.

THE CHARACTERS (PAGES 12–13)

Aim: to find textual evidence to build up knowledge of the characters.

Teaching points: this activity builds on the previous activity 'Maze talk'. A good starting point would be to review the classroom dialogue in Chapter 3. Read it aloud again. Ask children to brainstorm how they think each child feels about mazes based on the 'Maze talk' activity. At the same time you can talk about the illustrations and 'who has done what' so far in the story. Remind children that we learn about a character from what is said and what is done.

Extension: use drama activities to explore the relationships between the characters. The illustrations draw our attention to name-calling, Joe being laughed at and the children 'running rings round him'. Act out these scenes as small group role-play. You could use the 'freeze-frame' technique to explore what children are thinking, feeling and saying, or interview the characters by 'hot-seating' them.

RUNNING RINGS ROUND JOE (PAGE 14)

Aim: to explore Joe's character and feelings.

Teaching points: Joe sits under the table holding his key. He is hiding. At this point in the story we feel sorry for Joe. Akash, we are told, is not a bully, but Joe is certainly being picked on. It will be important to hold some class discussion on this in order to develop empathy with Joe as well as to raise some important school issues. If children have read Anne Fine's *The Angel of Nitshill Road* you will be able to make some comparisons. If not, use short picture books like *Willy the Wimp* or *Willy and Hugh* (both by Anthony Browne). See the 'Resources' section on page 28 for teacher resources on bullying.

Extension: children can write a letter from Joe's teacher to his parents explaining what has happened at school and how Joe can be helped. Children can work in groups to design a poster and leaflets for an anti-bullying campaign.

HOW IT ALL ENDS (PAGE 15)

The Snow Maze

Aim: to sequence the events that conclude the story.

Teaching points: the last two chapters are read together so that children can find out how the narrative resolves. Talk to the children about the way that the story develops. Highlight the events that lead from the maze as 'Joe's secret' to the maze as 'public property'. Children can work in groups to sequence the events, cutting out the boxes and pasting them onto a large sheet of paper. (This works best if you enlarge the photocopiable sheet.) The events can then be illustrated to provide a comic-strip version of the story ending.

Extension: children could think of alternative endings to the story. If there had been no frost or snow how might events have been resolved?

DEVELOPING IDEAS
A-MAZE-ING (PAGE 16)

Aim: to look at the use of symbols and illustration in building up the context of the story.

Teaching points: Jan Ormerod describes the maze theme as a 'visual gift'. She has drawn mazes throughout the book. Her drawings are based on a turf maze in Saffron Walden. The chapter heads represent the stages in constructing a unicursal maze. Remind the children what they learned about mazes when they did the activity 'Maze talk' on page 11. Explain to the children that the Snow Maze lettering on the front cover was created by the designer of the book not the illustrator. The illustrations help us to picture the maze and how its significance develops as the story unfolds.

Extension: children can draw their own mazes using the chapter headings as a guideline. They can also develop their own mazes in different media. Use the emblems at the chapter headings as templates for building a model maze with clay. Try to get support for making or painting a maze in the playground (see resources on page 28) – otherwise chalk will do! This can be developed into constructing larger scale mazes (see the Teachers' notes that refer to the activity 'Maze talk').

JOE'S FEELINGS (PAGE 17)

Aim: to develop empathy with the main character and look at how he changes in response to events in the narrative.

Teaching points: this activity looks at how events and the actions of others may have made Joe feel. Discuss the activity first. A good way in is to ask children to think about similar events in their own experience, how they felt and what they thought. At the bottom of the photocopiable sheet there is a bank of words that can be used to describe Joe's

feelings, so that children do not just write 'happy' or 'sad'. They can use these words or choose others.

Extension: build up a 'role-on-the-wall' poster for Joe. Use a large piece of paper and draw round a child to provide an outline of Joe. Inside the outline write down words or phrases that describe the type of person Joe is 'from the inside', for instance lonely, sad, secretive, imaginative. On the outside of the outline write words and phrases that describe the external Joe, for example what he looks like, what he does.

CHANGING RELATIONSHIPS (PAGES 18–19)

Aim: to look at the changing relationships between characters as the story develops.

Teaching points: the illustrator, Jan Ormerod, has picked up on a lot of the clues in the text. Ask the children to study carefully the illustrations that show Joe, Irrum and Akash. Their facial expressions communicate their feelings and attitudes to each other. Encourage children to draw on phrases from the text as well as the illustrations when they carry out this activity.

Extension: use the 'role-on-the-wall' technique (described in the Teachers' notes for the activity 'Joe's feelings', page 17) to explore what Akash thinks and feels at the midpoint of the story in Chapter 4, 'The Secret Maze', and what he thinks and feels at the end of the story.

IT COULDN'T HAPPEN HERE (PAGE 20)

Aim: to explore what we mean by fantasy by thinking about what is 'real' and what is 'imaginary' in the story.

Teaching points: this is not an easy concept to get across, since the story itself does not really have a basis in reality. However, there are such things as turf mazes, locked gates, and children called Joe and Akash. These may be familiar, whereas the idea of the maze being invisible to people unless they see it through the gate is unlikely in a literal sense. Follow this up with some discussion on what children think is 'magic' in this story and in others.

Extension: children can follow this up by thinking about a range of stories they all know and working out what is 'real' and what is 'imaginary' in them. This can be recorded in a simple two column table.

SHARING THE MAZE (PAGE 21)

Aim: to investigate a character's motivation from close reading and inference.

Teaching points: at first Joe keeps the maze secret and when Irrum asks to see it he refuses. Then he remembers what Irrum has said and done in the past. This is summarized towards the end of

Chapter 5 'The Invisible Maze' but you will need to encourage the children to find other sources of evidence. For instance, at the end of Chapter 1 Irrum suggests that the key might open the lonely gate. She sticks up for Joe on a number of occasions. Later on, when it snows, Irrum plays an important role in helping the others to run the maze.

Extension: Joe is reluctant to let others see the maze. In Chapter 6, 'The Frost Maze', Jan Mark writes: 'He wanted to be believed, but he wanted to keep his secret maze.' This is a critical point in the story. Sharing his secret is risky. Ask children to list the advantages and disadvantages of keeping the maze secret. The drama technique of a 'corridor-of-advice' can also be used. One child in role as Joe walks slowly between two rows of children. One row tries to persuade Joe to keep the maze a secret, while the other row tries to persuade him to share the secret. Children take it in turns to influence Joe as he walks past. The child playing Joe must then make a decision. (This technique may also sometimes be referred to as 'conscience-alley'.)

JOE'S SECRET DIARY (PAGE 22)

Aim: to develop empathy and insight into the central character and to retell events from a different point of view.

Teaching points: most children will be familiar with the diary form of writing, although you may wish to remind them through revisiting favourite stories such as Colin McNaughton's *Captain Abdul's Pirate School* or Michael Morpurgo's *The Wreck of the Zanzibar*. Children will have to be creative with the time-scale because there are few clues – although it is probably set in winter time!

Extension: some children may be keen on the secret diary theme and will want to write the earlier stages. Alternatively, they could write parts of Irrum's secret diary. The story could then be retold by reading selected extracts from both diaries.

MAZE TIME (PAGE 23)

Aim: to hypothesize about events before and after the story.

Teaching points: this activity requires children to speculate about events before and after the story. Some questions to prompt the children may be helpful, for instance: When was the turf maze first constructed? When did the wall fall down to leave the lonely gate? Who lost the key? When did they lose it? Were Akash and Joe friends before the story? What happened to the maze after the story? Did Irrum and Joe continue to be friends?

Extension: at the end of the story, Joe hides the key in the long grass. Ask children to write a story based on the rediscovery of the key.

PLOTTING EVENTS (PAGE 24)

Aim: to look at the story structure and sequence of events.

Teaching points: this activity helps children to order the events in the narrative. The activity works well collaboratively. The children may find it easier to paste the event boxes onto a large maze drawn on paper or card. (You will need to enlarge the event boxes.) They can discuss the order before pasting the boxes.

Extension: encourage children to retell the story using the 'story maze' they created in the main activity. They can use their finger or a pointer to work their way to the centre of the story maze. Storytellers can be invited to tell the story to other classes using this plan, and to practise their storytelling skills by taping them first onto a cassette recorder.

EVERY PICTURE TELLS A STORY (PAGE 25)

Aim: to interpret visual elements of the book and to understand how the illustrator extends the story.

Teaching points: Jan Ormerod adds to the story through her illustrations. The double page spreads in 'The Secret Maze' and 'The Frost Maze' chapters are a good example of this. In the first illustration Joe and Irrum stand still while the silhouetted figures of the others run round them. Joe is at the centre of this maze but Irrum is on the outside. In the second illustration all the children are shown as silhouettes as they run the maze in the snow.

Extension: children can draw their own pictures and add captions and dialogue in speech bubbles.

THINKING ABOUT *THE MAZE* (PAGE 26)

Aim: to reflect on the story in the light of comments from the author and illustrator.

Teaching points: the views of author and illustrator add to our interpretation of the text. Children can re-read or skim through the book after reading the quotes. Encourage them to relate their comments on 'what she means' to what happens in the book.

Extension: children can design a promotional leaflet to encourage others to read this book. This should include a brief plot summary and quotations from readers.

> Some run the Shepherd's Race – a rut
> Within a grass-plot deeply cut
> And wide enough to tread –
> A maze of path, of old designed
> To tire the feet' perplex the mind,
> Yet pleasure heart and head:
> 'Tis not unlike this life we spend,
> And where you start from, there you end
> *In Carol Shield's novel: 'Larry's Party' (Fourth Estate)*